PREPARING FOR TOMORROW'S CAREERS™

POWERING UP A CAREER IN
SOFTWARE
DEVELOPMENT
AND PROGRAMMING

DANIEL E. HARMON

ROSEN
PUBLISHING®

New York

Published in 2016 by The Rosen Publishing Group, Inc.
29 East 21st Street, New York, NY 10010

Library of Congress Cataloging-in-Publication Data

Harmon, Daniel E., author.
Powering up a career in software development and programming/Daniel E.
Harmon.
    pages cm.—(Preparing for tomorrow's careers)
ISBN 978-1-4994-6095-7 (library bound)
1. Computer software—Development—Vocational guidance—Juvenile
literature. 2. Information technology—Vocational guidance—Juvenile
literature. [1. Vocational guidance.] I. Title.
QA76.76.D47H367 2016
005.1'2023—dc23

                                                        2014042226

Manufactured in the United States of America

CONTENTS

Introduction   4

CHAPTER ONE
TECHNOLOGY THAT DAZZLES   8

CHAPTER TWO
PREPARE NOW FOR YOUR CAREER   15

CHAPTER THREE
CAREERS IN SOFTWARE DEVELOPMENT   25

CHAPTER FOUR
CAREERS IN PROGRAMMING   34

CHAPTER FIVE
CAREERS IN RELATED FIELDS   43

CHAPTER SIX
LANDING A JOB   55

CHAPTER SEVEN
WIDE-OPEN OPPORTUNITIES   62

Glossary   68
For More Information   70
For Further Reading   73
Bibliography   75
Index   78

INTRODUCTION

Software developers and programmers are vital players in the realm of computers and information technology (IT). The creative minds behind the screens, they build the programs and systems that tell the hardware what to do, driving much of what people then do in today's tech-intensive world.

Scarcely a day goes by when an individual's life is not impacted by computer programming. This fact is especially true in the lives of young adults, teens, and even children under age ten. Using their smartphones, tablets, laptops, or desktops, these thirty-somethings and younger spend much of every day fixed to a screen. They rely on technology for communicating and networking—texting, e-mailing, videochatting, tweeting, and connecting on Facebook, as well as other social-networking platforms. A 2012 survey conducted for the Badoo social network indicated that 39 percent of

Preparation for a programming or software-development career can begin early. These high school students are working to create an iPad app that tracks hall passes electronically.

Americans spend more time socializing online. In 2013, *Business News Daily* reported findings that in the course of a week, the typical American spends twenty-three hours—almost a full day—on the Internet or texting.

And that's only the beginning. Much of today's popular entertainment is available onscreen or online. Photos, videos, and music are recorded digitally, and software makes it a cinch to enhance, alter, and combine media files. Rather than create art by hand, many artistic individuals now prefer to express themselves with digital creations, which can instantly be shared online.

Students also rely on computers for schoolwork. Internet sources provide information for all kinds of projects. Word processors facilitate typing and catch spelling and grammatical errors. Math utilities perform quick calculations. Programs and online educational resources make learning more enjoyable, providing content that's rich with colorful illustrations and videos. A side benefit of our increasingly computer-centric world is that IT has helped move society toward a paperless state, and paper reduction is good for the environment.

People of all ages use their smartphones to obtain directions to destinations. They get instant updates on news, weather, local traffic conditions, sports scores and standings, and much more.

Advertisers are shifting their campaigns to online media. As a result, consumers increasingly learn about new products via the Internet—where they also can find instant reviews and alerts.

Finally, computer technology has dramatically changed the way society exchanges money. From million-dollar business deals to pizza delivery orders, countless financial transactions occur every minute that involve no physical currency. More and more workers have their paychecks deposited automatically into their checking accounts. They do much or most of their spending electronically, too. Gartner, Inc., a major research firm, estimates that 245 million people were making mobile payments in 2013. Gartner projected the number to rise to 450 million in 2017.

Where do you fit into this picture? All of these capabilities can be credited to the time and talents of gifted software developers and programmers—people who develop the technology that makes each task possible. If you're interested in joining their ranks, this book is a first step toward planning your future.

Jobs in this arena are diverse. Some technical professionals who work freelance or for small software companies function as both developer and programmer. This is particularly the case in the creation of simple apps. Most software, though, is the work of development and programming teams that may require dozens or hundreds of professionals.

Whatever their role and work environment, software technologists are engaged in highly rewarding work in terms of income as well as contributions to society. Software development and programming offer one of the most open and exciting career fields in the twenty-first century. Read on to discover more about the world behind the screens.

CHAPTER ONE

TECHNOLOGY THAT DAZZLES

A hiker with a scout troop strays from the others. An hour later, with foul weather setting in, the absent scout has not returned. An alert is issued.

Computer technology pinpoints where the wanderer was last seen. A program analyzes the area's terrain, vegetation, elevations, angles, and other factors. Where, considering all those variables, was the lost scout most likely to proceed?

The result is a happy ending. The hiker is located, safe and unhurt.

Can a computer program really help find missing people? There just might be "an app for that," or that kind of problem. Computer programs serve us in many ways. They can do things that weren't possible a generation ago.

Let's say you're listening to a song on the radio while riding to school. You'd like to download it but you have no idea of the title or recording artist. With the right app, you can record a snatch of it with your smart phone. The app makes a "sound print" of the music, searches for a match in a song database, and gives you the information.

Computer programs today can quickly analyze the findings of medical tests. They can foretell with proven accuracy the likelihood that a financial investment will succeed or fail. They can find you jobs in your interest and specialty area at nearby places of employment. They can guide you through yoga and other physical and mental exercises while seated at a workstation. They can defeat most human chess masters. They can find you a shortcut across town when you're in a hurry.

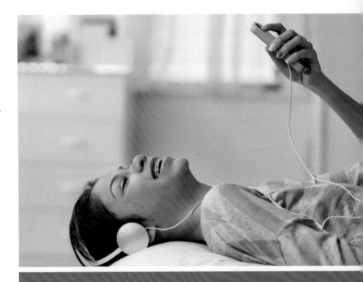

Using an app such as SoundHound, listeners can verify their guesses as to the title or artist of a song that's being played. Software developers and programmers make this form of entertainment possible.

In the old days, contact management utilities stored the names, phone numbers, and addresses of people with whom we regularly communicated. Today's contact programs, using social network data, can tell us when and where we met the person *and* list our mutual friends.

Weather service apps give us hourly predictions of weather in our local areas. Now, advanced apps are predicting weather by the *minute*.

Who makes all this mind-boggling computer technology possible? Millions of dedicated professionals are involved, most notably the software developers and the programmers who convey their ideas into workable applications.

A TREASURE TROVE OF MIGHTY SOFTWARE

Mobile apps are the most visible and exciting products of development and programming. New apps are constantly introduced. They can perform simple and complex tasks. They can help save lives—or waste hours of time playing mindless games.

It's been calculated that new apps are launched every minute of the day. Many of them merely duplicate what's already on the market. Others are designed for obscure tasks that mean little to most people. A few, though, prove themselves truly useful to thousands of consumers.

Can an app help people relax, de-stress, and meditate on positive thoughts? In September 2014, a company called Zen180 launched an app through the Apple iTunes store designed for users to "get focused, creative, and help with everyday stresses of living." Background music can be chosen for a specific purpose—relaxing, reading, or doing homework. "The idea is to listen to the audio track with headphones while you are trying to focus on a task or simply to meditate," the vendor explains.

While small-screen apps garner much of the attention in the popular media, larger, more powerful computer programs lie underneath many of the changes in the way people live and work. Computer technology is being applied to long-range projects in numerous industries and professions: scientific, automotive, medical, energy-related, environmental, military, and others. Examples range from voice-activated devices and systems in cars and

Mobile apps such as Zen180 can help listeners relax and destress while enjoying their music. App developers today explore new ways to make old technology more beneficial.

homes to the remote control of drone aircraft and space telescopes. Work on some of these technologies has taken many years and involved thousands of computer professionals.

Some software endeavors never succeed. In such cases, after weeks, months, or even years of exhaustive programming, testing, trial, and error, project managers must acknowledge the objective cannot be attained. But does that mean all the time and work were lost? Dedicated software developers and programmers say no. To paraphrase U.S. inventor Thomas A. Edison (1847–1931), they haven't failed; they've simply tested and exposed another way that doesn't work.

MAKING VOICES MORE POWERFUL

An especially exciting area of programming is in voice technology. Software innovations have given the spoken word far greater power today than ever before.

Busy executives once dictated letters, reports, and other documents to secretaries who typed and distributed them. The introduction of tape recorders for dictation freed secretaries to handle more pressing tasks and process the dictated material later. Small, portable dictation devices let people draft documents wherever they happened to be, not confined to their offices.

Now, software converts dictation to text automatically. It also works in the opposite direction, speaking typed text aloud in an electronic voice. This function allows people to "read" (hear) news and entertainment articles, books, and business or school documents when they can't sit down and read, such as when driving, bicycling, or walking. Such technology is also invaluable to the blind, giving them easy access to much of the written material that once had to be read to them.

Advances in voice technology continue to unfold. Already, programs allow people to speak to their mobile phones and computers, obtaining directions and information without having to type their requests. With voice bio-metric capability, computers can recognize an individual's voice, not merely the words that are being spoken. This capacity enables automated call centers at banks, for example, to verify the identity of a caller without the need for a password (which can be stolen). Voice biometrics can also be useful in criminal investigations.

FANTASTIC ENTERTAINMENT

With the latest game and entertainment programs and apps, Internet users interact with large or small screens. They indulge in diversions that people thirty years ago couldn't even imagine. Here are just a few examples of what's out there:

- Streaming movies and audio connections, which can be accessed with a few touches on a mobile device
- Music recordings of the past seventy to eighty years
- Auto racing games in which players maneuver at blinding speeds against competitors in assorted vehicles—complete with aerial stunts
- Online participation in classic games such as Monopoly and chess, playing with opponents who may reside in distant countries

Tomb Raider is one of thousands of science fiction video games popular among young people. Programmers can have fun creating lucrative products for the entertainment market.

- Lethal combat engagements, from hand-to-hand clashes to secret airborne missions to global and interplanetary warfare using sci-fi weaponry

All of these consumer pleasures are made possible by developers and programmers.

CHAPTER TWO

PREPARE NOW FOR YOUR CAREER

Y ou don't have to wait until high school graduation to begin scoping out career possibilities in software development and programming; you can investigate how software and mobile apps work while still in high school or middle school. Some students are already writing game programs for their personal enjoyment. With an app development kit, you can dabble in app programming. By the time you cross the stage to receive your diploma, you can already have significant experience.

Even if you have little knowledge about software, you can concentrate on courses that will be the foundation of your further education. STEM classes (science, technology, engineering, and math) are central. Technology and math are particularly important. Computer science classes are essential. Depending on your specific interest, other areas of study may also be important in your preparation.

Teenagers are developing cool apps—and some (well, a handful, at least) have made it into the mainstream of app development.

15

DIFFERENT APPROACHES TO DIFFERENT CAREER PATHS

The elective courses you choose, club involvement, part-time employment, volunteer services, and other activities will be guided by your career interest. Consider these three related but different examples.

- A young person aspires to design a future-generation computer operating system or productivity software suite. This goal will require knowledge of almost all aspects of computer technology. The earlier the basic education begins, the better.
- Another student is fascinated by creating snazzy websites and pages, using eye- and ear-catching devices including graphics, text art, photo collages, and video and music streams. This interest assumes artistic and other creative talent as well as computer know-how.
- A student has a passion for problem solving. Software installation, troubleshooting, and maintenance would seem a likely career prospect.

SCHOLARSHIPS

Scholarships are funded by corporations, individuals, and higher-learning institutions. Some are very competitive, awarded to high school graduates ranked near the head of their class. Others are awarded based on financial need.

Jeremy Harrison, a University of Cincinnati systems administrator who provides descriptions and pointers to dozens of available scholarships at his *Computer Science Zone* career blog, writes: "Students working toward a degree in computer science have a long list of scholarship options ranging from private groups to government agencies."

But "don't stop here," Harrison advises students. "Companies across the world are looking for people with degrees in computer science and other related technologies. The industry is growing fast and shows no signs of slowing down. . . . There are more scholarships and grants offered each year to support the need

Teams of college students vie in national and international programming contests. Some competitions are sponsored by leading technology corporations—a special incentive for inventive minds.

for increased numbers of skilled workers, creators, and designers."

EARLY OPPORTUNITIES

While in high school and college, teenagers can apply for internships and participate in work-study programs. Some internships pay substantial salaries and provide housing, meals, transportation, and recreational benefits.

Opportunities are available in different branches of this overall career field. The following internship examples are typical.

SOFTWARE DEVELOPMENT

A small software company in New York City hires four software development interns each summer and puts them to work on "real shipping software." They are involved in developing and upgrading both desktop

COMPUTER LINGO

Please do check out the glossary in the back, but here is a mini-glossary devoted to computer languages, programs, and the like:

BASIC The acronym for beginner's all-purpose symbolic instruction code, BASIC is a simplified language for programming and interacting with a computer.

C A general-purpose computer language developed in the early 1970s at the telephone company originally started by inventor Alexander Graham Bell.

C++ Pronounced *cee plus plus*, this language is like C with the added feature of allowing for a certain amount of computer memory manipulation.

CSS3 The acronym for cascading style sheets, this version of CSS uses modules (separate documents) to describe the look of a document written in markup language.

Dreamweaver Application used to create websites and apps on various devices (e.g., tablets, smartphones).

HTML5 The acronym for hypertext markup language, this version of HTML is the standard programming web-coding language used to describe the contents and appearance of webpages.

Java This programming language allows programmers to write computer instructions in words (say, in English) rather than in numeric codes.

Markup language This overall language of the Web includes "sub" languages such as HTML and XML.

Scripting language (e.g., Lua, Perl, Python) This programming language allows control of one or more software applications.

The Cloud These are software and services than run on the Internet, not on a personal storage device such as a computer.

XML The acronym for extensible markup language, XML is a document-formatting language used for some webpages.

and mobile applications. Interns are regarded as temporary employees with major responsibilities, not as "just interns."

While working, interns are mentored by experienced team members. This relationship gives students the opportunity to learn about software development, code testing, and designing user interfaces from experts. The interns also work with documentation, marketing, and customer support.

Most interns are between their junior and senior years of college with computer science coursework behind them (although they need not be CS majors). They must have excellent grades and programming skills. The interview process includes solving coding problems.

The organization boasts: "Our summer internship program allows talented college students to learn about the software industry from the inside in the most exciting city in the world."

PROGRAMMING

Gaming software companies may hire game-programming interns. Interns are bachelor's and master's degree candidates in the fields of computer science, computer engineering, mathematics, game programming, or similar curricula. They should have experience programming games, either professionally or personally, working in the C and C++ languages. They should be familiar with a scripting language such as Lua, Perl, or Python and understand game-play logic, artificial intelligence, content creation, pathing, compression, and encryption.

Candidates for gaming internships need to be strong in math and understand algorithms and data structures. They have an advantage if they are also knowledgeable in the use of Microsoft Visual Studio, plugins, animation, sounds, and networking. Naturally, they have a passion for computer games as well as for programming. Interns work closely with staff program designers and artists who share their zeal.

Interns benefit greatly from this experience—and so does the company. Interns debug and improve existing game code. They play-test programs that are in development and help ensure that the game features and program tools work properly.

SOFTWARE SUPPORT

A Massachusetts software development company employs five paid support interns year-round. The company develops business management programs for systems planning and customer relationships for companies and organizations across North America.

Software support interns assist the firm's developers. They deal with customer support and help troubleshoot code problems. The ideal intern candidates are skilled in basic programming and understand web applications. Further training in those areas is provided onsite.

WEB DESIGN AND DEVELOPMENT

An international publishing company uses a graphic web design intern to create, develop, and maintain attractive websites. The intern also develops signage, logos, and other promotional materials for the company and its affiliates.

The intern must be experienced in design software such as Adobe InDesign, Photoshop, and Illustrator. The work includes layout design, illustration, and photo manipulation. The intern also uses HTML5, Dreamweaver, and CSS3 to create user-friendly websites.

Besides knowledge of technical tools, the intern needs a thorough understanding of color management and typography. The work requires a creative mind and an eye for detail.

Dreamweaver is a popular platform for creating websites. Students exploring a career focused on website development should acquaint themselves with tools used by web professionals.

FOCUS ON COMPUTER STUDIES

Students interested in computer software careers can focus their time and studies on technology, math, and related subjects while in high school. They should become active in computer clubs in school or in the community. Visits to local web design or computer support firms can yield valuable advice and insight into the technology workplace.

EXAMINE THE JOB MARKET

An excellent, easy way to find out what skills and education you'll need for a career in software development or programming is to conduct a simple Internet job search using those and related terms. You'll find current job listings with detailed descriptions of the work, environment, required education and experience, and beginning pay.

You'll probably also find job listings for specific as well as related jobs. A search for "software developer jobs" may turn up openings for applications engineers, quality engineers, test engineers, mobile software engineers, and developers who specialize in certain programming languages such as Java. A search for "web developer jobs" will likely bring up listings for entry-level web developers, front-end web developers, freelance web developers, and professionals who function as both web marketers and developers.

You can narrow your search to obtain particular job details. For example, you can search for "computer programming jobs in [your city or state]," "computer programming jobs entry level," "computer programming jobs from home," "computer programming jobs outlook," or "computer programming jobs salary."

While you're at it, look for available student internships. Even though you may not be ready to apply for an internship, you might be surprised at the opportunities that are out there. It is also wise to know what's down the road so that you can sign up for the appropriate classes in school.

Programming and software design projects for school science fairs not only are instructive but may also catch the attention of industry and college representatives. These connections can lead to scholarships or internships.

School guidance counselors help students investigate and compare related career paths. They point students to college or technical school programs and possible scholarships. Counselors are acquainted with local employers in different fields.

CHAPTER THREE

CAREERS IN SOFTWARE DEVELOPMENT

When personal computers became popular in the 1980s, many users were frustrated. The machines they were buying seemed powerful, but useful program applications seemed limited. Science- and math-minded consumers began writing their own programs to perform specific tasks. They used early languages such as BASIC and C. Some of the do-it-yourself programming geeks came up with applications that could benefit not just themselves but masses of people. A few managed to interest fledgling software companies in their work. A handful even launched their own companies.

Gone are those days when bleary-eyed, self-taught programmers sat up late at home, meticulously crafting lines of program code. Most software today is developed by teams, in stages. Software developers conceive what they want a new product to accomplish. The concept then goes to programmers to bring it to life. The developer oversees and controls the process.

WHAT SOFTWARE DEVELOPERS DO

The Bureau of Labor Statistics' *Occupational Outlook Handbook* describes developers as "the creative minds behind computer programs." Some of them (systems software developers) devise elaborate systems that will control an organization's networks and run its computers. Others (applications software developers) develop software that will perform specific tasks.

Developers are hired by companies, agencies, or individuals who need computer technology to perform a task or group of related tasks for their line of business. Developers create flowcharts to guide programmers

A software developer presents his app that allows builders to examine floor plans and related building data. Such apps are informative and helpful for architects, contractors, and others.

in writing software code. Before they can devise an effective flowchart, though, there is much work to do. To understand exactly what the client wants and needs, developers confer at length with the client or corporate officials. Developers then set to work designing a system that will meet those needs, discussing the project with various computer specialists in order to arrive at the most effective design.

Most software consists of many linked components. Developers design each part and plan how everything will function as a whole. They carefully document details of how the program is to function. As each segment of a program is written, beta testers (testers of software while it's under development) try it out. They look for design flaws and areas for improvement before software is installed for the client's use or released to consumers. The designers make sure the application works as intended.

Even then, the developers' role is not finished. Most software is a perpetual work in progress. Reviewers and end users report things that they dislike about the program. Based on feedback, developers suggest upgrades and changes. This process generally continues until support for the product is discontinued and it is taken off the market.

SYSTEMS DEVELOPERS

Systems software developers design the software that runs computers, phones, tablets, cars, and other items. Systems software includes operating systems—Windows, iOS, Android, etc. It also includes software that drives computer systems specially developed for a given company, government agency, or other large organization. Some systems developers design the system interface—the control screen the user needs in order to work the device.

APPLICATIONS DEVELOPERS

Computer applications are programs developed for end users. Applications (usually called apps) range from sophisticated word processors and tax preparation programs to games and apps for accessing weather and GPS services. Some apps are developed for general use. Others are designed to enable a single organization to carry out a unique internal task.

Increasingly, apps are developed for use in the cloud. That means they will not be installed on an end user's computer or mobile device but will reside on a remote server. A server is a central computer to which consumers can connect and use online.

IT PROJECT MANAGERS

In some cases, developers assume the role of information technology project managers. A manager is in overall charge of a software development project, from early planning through programming, testing, and installation. The manager is involved in defining the organization's IT objectives and establishing technology budgets. He or she ensures that a project is completed successfully, on schedule, and within the approved budget. The manager also oversees information and network security issues.

EFFECTIVE DEVELOPMENT TAKES TIME

Hundreds of thousands of apps are available for mobile devices, and new ones are introduced daily. Some are designed to accomplish fast, simple tasks. Others are complex, able to perform multiple functions.

How long does it take to develop a useful mobile app? Some app specialists have created functional apps in a few hours. Most apps, however, take weeks or months. Adam Zolyak, project manager at Seque Technologies

(continued on the next page)

University students present their app in a programming competition. Sophisticated mobile apps may take only hours to develop . . . or months.

(continued from the previous page)

(www.seguetech.com), explained the process in an article posted on the company's blog. Typically, Zolyak wrote, the initial build of an app takes the project team at least three months. Apps with advanced capabilities can take more than six months to perfect.

Zolyak divided his time estimates into stages:

- Planning (which he dubbed "envisioning"): two to four weeks
- Developing and testing by the project team: six to eight weeks
- Stabilization (incorporating client feedback and making sure the app is compatible with mobile devices): one to two weeks

When the app is ready for market, the project team assists the client in launching it at an online store. This process can take another two weeks.

By contrast, major software projects take much, much longer. For example, when Microsoft introduces a new version of Windows or of its Office productivity suite, the next version is already well under development. That version may be several years from release to the consuming public.

Some IT project managers are put in charge of an entire IT department. They decide what personnel are needed permanently and per project. Department managers may supervise software developers, systems analysts, security specialists, and computer support staff.

WHERE THE DEVELOPMENT JOBS ARE

About a third of developers work with computer systems design firms and related services. Others work for electronic product makers, software publishers, and service industries such as finance and insurance.

Developers typically work in offices, collaborating with other members of a design, development, and programming team. Some are able to perform much of their work by telecommuting from offices at home. Hours can be long when under pressure to meet deadlines. On average, more than a fourth of developers put in more than forty hours a week.

JOB REQUIREMENTS

Most software developers have a bachelor's degree in computer science or a related subject such as software engineering or mathematics. Some have master's degrees. College programs in computer science require courses in all the necessary subtopics. A focus is on software building.

Many developers begin as programmers. As developers, they need to understand code in various programming languages.

Developers who work for specific industries and professions need to be intimately familiar with how the industry works. This foundational knowledge is vital to understanding the exact technology needs of their employers.

A PROMISING CAREER FIELD

According to the U.S. Department of Labor's Bureau of Labor Statistics, as of 2012 there were slightly more than a million professional software developers in the United States. As the field is rapidly expanding, almost a quarter-million more developer jobs are predicted by 2022. The projected growth rate of 22 percent is far faster than the growth rates for most other careers. The reason for such expansion is the global demand for new software. Key areas of growth are mobile applications, technology for the increasingly complex health care industry, and security software to counter cybercrime such as hacking. For systems software developers, the future is especially exciting because new technology is being introduced not just for traditional computers but for automobiles, aircraft, and appliances as well.

Software development is a lucrative career, paying almost three times the average income for all jobs tracked by the Bureau of Labor Statistics. Naturally, new jobs and advancement prospects will favor applicants who are skilled in up-to-date design and development techniques and different programming languages.

Developers may advance to become IT directors, IT security directors, and ultimately chief technology officers (CTOs).

DO YOU HAVE A FUTURE IN SOFTWARE DEVELOPMENT?

Software developers must have a combination of skills. Obviously, excellent computer skills are essential, including a knowledge of programming. Developers also need creative instincts. They must be able to analyze their employers' technology needs, design effective software, and communicate the development plan clearly to programmers and other team members. They must be effective problem solvers.

Other important strengths include attention to detail, the ability to multitask, and interpersonal skills. Developers are expected to work well with team members. They should be able to answer questions from their employers as well as people who will be using the program.

CHAPTER FOUR

CAREERS IN PROGRAMMING

Working closely with a client, developers come up with a detailed plan for new software. Programmers then set to work. Programmers take the developers' design and turn it into reality. They use programming languages such as Java and C++ to build sets of instructions for computers to run.

The work up front—writing program code—is only the beginning of the process. Debugging and upgrading are ongoing tasks that require programmers' efforts for as long as the program is in popular use.

Some program writing, notably for mobile apps, is simple and takes no more than a few days or weeks to complete. At the other extreme are long-range projects such as new versions of operating systems and office suites. These tasks might take years and involve large teams of programmers, developers, and other technologists.

WHAT SOFTWARE PROGRAMMERS DO

In some organizations, software development and programming overlap: developers might also be

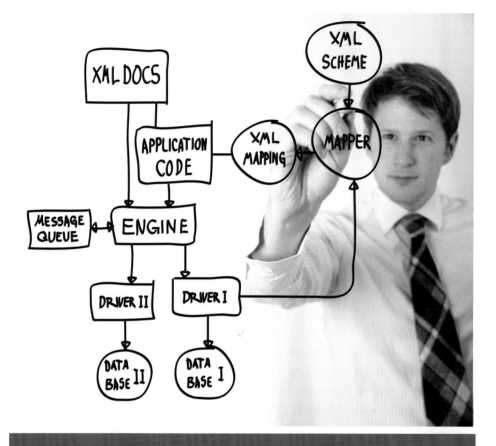

A software programmer diagrams XML coding structure. Programmers take the plans of software developers and make them into functional software for computers and other electronic devices.

programmers and vice versa. In any case, developers and programmers work together.

Programmers write the lines of code that tell computers how to run the software that developers conceive. They write code in a programming language that makes little sense to a nonprogrammer. Thousands of programming languages have been invented since the first electronic computers appeared in the 1940s. Some of the most common languages today include Java, JavaScript, C, C++, C#, HTML5, SQL, XML, Eclipse, Perl, and Python. PHP and CSS are popular with programmers who work with websites. New, experimental programming languages are frequently introduced. Much of a programmer's writing can be simplified with code libraries, which are blocks of code lines that are repeated frequently.

After a program is written, the programmer's work continues. Debugging is the process of testing a program and correcting any part that does not function properly. Upgrading means revising a program after it is in use, making improvements suggested by the program owner and end users.

More and more software today operates in the cloud. It runs on a computer to which the end user connects via the Internet. Traditionally, software has been written to run on users' individual computers, which are equipped with a particular operating system (mainly Microsoft's Windows or Apple's OSX). Cloud software, by contrast, is programmed to work with any computer the user has, regardless of its operating system.

Programmers typically work regular, full-time jobs in the offices of computer systems design firms or in corporate technology offices. For the most part, they do their work independently, although they may be members of teams who include multiple programmers, developers, and other technology professionals. While writing code, some programmers can telecommute from workstations set up at home or in their own private offices.

The least favorite part of the work for many programmers is writing descriptions of what they are coding. Joel Spolsky, renowned for his "Joel Test" for programmers, explains, "Most programmers hate writing documents. As a result, when teams consisting solely of programmers attack a problem, they prefer to express their solution in code, rather than in documents. They would much rather dive in and write code than produce a spec first."

A software requirement specification, or "spec,"

In 2000, noted software engineer and writer Joel Spolsky developed a rather quaint test to rate the efficiency of software programmers. Although somewhat outdated now, it remains a valuable gauge for aspiring technologists.

lays out in advance exactly what the program will do. It also explains to the client certain things the program will not do. Among other benefits, this

THE "JOEL" TEST FOR PROGRAMMERS

In 2000, Joel Spolsky published "The Joel Test: 12 Steps to Better Code." What he described as "my own, highly irresponsible, sloppy test to rate the quality of a software team" caught on in the programming community. Spolsky, a former Microsoft program manager, proposed twelve guideline questions programmers should ask themselves:

1. Do you use source control?
2. Can you make a build in one step?
3. Do you make daily builds?
4. Do you have a bug database?
5. Do you fix bugs before writing new code?
6. Do you have an up-to-date schedule?
7. Do you have a spec?
8. Do programmers have quiet working conditions?
9. Do you use the best tools money can buy?
10. Do you have testers?
11. Do new candidates write code during their interview?
12. Do you do hallway usability testing?

Hallway usability testing, Spolsky explained, "is where you grab the next person that passes by in the hallway and force them to try to use the code you just wrote. If you do this to five people, you will learn 95 percent of what there is to learn about usability problems in your code."

Recent critics have contended that while much of the "Joel Test" remains important, parts of it are no longer as relevant as they once were. Still, programmers pay heed to guidelines.

clarification heads off any misunderstandings that might arise between the client and the programming team.

WHAT DOES IT TAKE TO BE A GOOD PROGRAMMER?

Students who aspire to become software programmers obviously should be interested in most if not all of the STEM classroom subjects (science, technology, engineering, math) in high school. In addition, four personal traits are vital for computer programmers.

- Analytical skills. Developers give programmers detailed instructions to follow. Programmers must accurately analyze those guidelines and transform them into workable computer code.

- Attention to detail. A single typo in a single line (among thousands of lines) of code can render the program useless.
- Troubleshooting ability. When a problem arises (as software glitches always do), the programmer must be able to locate the cause and fix it as quickly as possible.
- Concentration. Programmers are often glued to their computer screens, writing code, many hours at a time, for days on end. They must be able to tune out distractions.

Programmers must be completely focused on their work in order to minimize glitches in code. Among other requirements, the "Joel Test" calls for quiet working conditions.

PROGRAMMING JOB REQUIREMENTS

High school and college students can begin acquiring programming experience through internships with local or regional companies or organizations. Some programmers obtain only an associate's degree from a technical college, although most have bachelor's degrees in computer science or related fields.

A key hiring factor is the applicant's proficiency in the programming language or languages that are most vital in the employing firm's projects. Experienced programmers are familiar with many languages, but they specialize in only a few. Most computer science programs in college equip students to learn new languages quickly.

Once established in their careers, programmers can earn certification in certain languages or software applications. Certified status may be useful for advancement.

Programmers who decide to specialize in one industry or service area—health care, finance, or automotive, for example—can improve their employment prospects by taking courses to educate themselves in the general subject. They need to understand the issues and special challenges of people who work in that field in order to produce the most effective programs.

Many creators of mobile apps have no degrees or formal training (although some have bachelor's and higher degrees). However, they have to be intimately knowledgeable about how mobile devices operate and how users interact with them. Besides general computing skills, app programmers need to know the programming languages used for the mobile operating platform they're working with (such as Android, iOS, Windows Mobile, Blackberry, or Symbian).

A DIGITAL WORLD OF OPPORTUNITY

Most programmers earn above the average pay for all jobs. Overall, the number of new programming jobs is expected to increase by about 8 percent between now and 2022—about the average rate of all job growth. Growth is expected to be higher for jobs in cloud and mobile app programming.

Beginning a career as a software programmer does not mean you will spend your life typing lines of obscure code into a computer. Some programmers move on to jobs as software developers, IT managers, systems analysts, and related positions.

In any career field related to computer technology, workers are expected to stay abreast of new developments. Some cutting-edge programs and systems five or ten years ago are obsolete today. Advancement prospects will be best for those who learn new programming tools. Ambitious programmers learn emerging programming languages and attend programs and seminars to stay up to date.

CHAPTER FIVE

CAREERS IN RELATED FIELDS

J obs related to software development and programming regularly overlap. For that reason, young people interested in the overall field should be aware of the wide range of possible careers. Here are some examples.

COMPUTER SYSTEMS ANALYSIS

Systems analysts examine a business's or organization's computer systems and setup, looking for ways to improve operations. They have a solid understanding of business needs and a thorough knowledge of computer technology.

Computer systems analysts are employed in various businesses, professions, and industries. More than a fourth of them work for computer systems design firms and associated services. Others work in finance, insurance, and government management and information. Some analysts work under contract as consultants; others are regular employees.

Analysts work closely with the company's or agency's systems managers. They must understand precisely the organization's information technology needs. Analysts consider every technology available to improve or replace the firm's existing systems. They draw up a detailed cost and benefit analysis. Their findings help organization leaders determine whether an upgrade or replacement will be worth the expense.

Analysts are then involved in designing and acquiring the hardware and software needed for a new system, overseeing the setup and installation. Quality assurance analysts test the systems. Other analysts write instructions and help train users. Analysts known as IT project managers are in charge of the installation or upgrade process at every stage. Systems analysts regularly collaborate with other professionals. They sometimes travel to distant employer locations.

Analysts need excellent math skills. They calculate, for example, the speed and amount of memory a planned system must have. They know programming languages and often engage in the programming process. Because they work with both business managers and technology specialists, they need good communication skills. They must be able to explain technical details to business managers and business needs to technical professionals.

A college education is not required for all analyst jobs, but most systems analysts hold bachelor's degrees or technical school degrees in subjects related to computer science or information technology. Some have master's degrees. In addition, business and management courses are helpful, since most jobs combine computer and business expertise. Some analysts hold degrees in business or other nontechnical areas; they also have training and experience in programming or information technology.

The job outlook is superb, predicted to grow 25 percent by 2022. The reason for the rapid growth is society's increasing reliance on information technology in businesses, industries, and government agencies.

To improve advancement opportunities, analysts take courses to educate themselves about new technology. They may eventually become team leaders, project managers, and IT directors or chief technology officers.

COMPUTER SOFTWARE SUPPORT

Support specialists are hired or contracted by firms to help workers use computers and software more effectively. Support staff work in various industries and professions, including education, finance, information technology, telecommunication, and health care. They train workers, answer questions, and resolve problems. Network support specialists assist the organization's IT employees. User support specialists work with nontechnical users.

Duties vary, depending on the kind of support assigned to the specialist. Some support professionals test and maintain network systems. They troubleshoot problems with local, wide area, and Internet networks. In most organizations, network support specialists are part of the IT staff.

Having a problem with your computer or mobile device? Support specialists are on call 24/7 to assist. They must have intimate knowledge of the systems they represent.

User support specialists sometimes are referred to as help desk technicians. Much of their work is done by phone, e-mail, or online chat. Some of it is done onsite. They diagnose customers' problems and walk them through the solutions. They sometimes install or help users install software. Some specialists train customers to use new software. Support specialists might work normal schedules or be required to be available after hours, twenty-four hours a day, as problems arise.

Support specialists need excellent problem solving skills. They are good listeners and patient in working with users who are frustrated by software problems. Good communication skills, both verbal and written, are important.

Computer support specialists may have different backgrounds in education and experience. Network support specialists usually have associate's or bachelor's degrees in computer-related studies. User support jobs may not require a degree but rather computer knowledge and perhaps the completion of computer courses at a technical school. Support jobs with software companies usually call for a bachelor's degree in computer or information science or engineering.

Support specialists take continuing education in new technology to improve advancement opportunities. Besides advancing in support areas, they may progress to jobs as software developers or system administrators.

Job growth in computer support is expected to be approximately 17 percent by 2022. Many new jobs will be in the realm of cloud computing.

WEB DEVELOPMENT, DESIGN, AND MAINTENANCE

Developers and programmers who are especially intrigued by how people interact with the Internet may devote themselves to website development and maintenance. Besides programming knowledge, website creation requires graphic-design talent. Some developers design websites and work on an entire project from planning to launch. Others are hired to create and maintain site sections and pages.

Web developers are in charge not only of how a site appears onscreen but how well it performs. Performance factors include easy-to-follow site organization, the speed of navigating from one section of the site to another, and the ease of linking to related Internet resources. Web developers must make versions of the site workable on the small screens of mobile devices. Some developers create content (text, graphics, video) as well as designing and building the site.

Is computer work a one-person/one-screen routine? Rarely. Whatever their roles, professionals involved in computer design and programming regularly have multiple computer screens in front of them.

During the early years of Internet growth in the 1990s, many website creators were self-taught. They either learned the HTML web coding language and built sites line by line or bought off-the-shelf software to create simple websites and pages.

Most web developers today have associate's or bachelor's degrees in web design, graphic design, programming, or a related area. More technical roles may require a further degree. A high school diploma is enough for some jobs, though, if the developer has sufficient computer knowledge, creative talent, and experience.

According to the Bureau of Labor Statistics, about a fourth of web developers work for themselves. Most work full-time; those in business for themselves may put in many hours of overtime to become established. Others work for small development firms, for computer systems design services, or for different professions and industries, organizations, and government agencies.

Job prospects are good, especially for professionals who can work with multiple programming languages and creativity software. A 20-percent growth in the job market is expected in coming years—much higher than for all jobs monitored by the Bureau of Labor Statistics. Web professionals with bachelor's degrees can advance to roles as web project managers or IT managers.

Important personal qualities for pursuing a career in web work include creativity and the ability to concentrate in distracting work environments. Webmasters must be able to communicate well with clients and understand what will impress visitors to

TIPS FOR STUDENTS FROM A WEB DESIGN PRO

In 2002, when Banks Wilson launched Studiobanks, a small web design firm in Charlotte, North Carolina, he did most of the work himself. He was optimistic his fledgling enterprise would grow over time—but little did he imagine how vastly it would expand or the changes it would undergo.

Wilson obtained a bachelor of fine arts degree with a graphic design focus and soon after graduation started his agency. Early on, he mostly focused on web design. He soon found that many of his clients needed more than effective websites to promote their businesses and brands. In response, he began offering other digital services, such as marketing via search engines, social media, and e-mail.

In 2014, he rebranded his firm as UNION (www.union.co), a full-service digital marketing agency with twenty professionals on staff. Included are digital designers, strategists, account managers, copywriters, and technologists. Staffers craft digital marketing platforms, content, and campaigns for major corporations and organizations. The new name, Wilson explains, reflects the agency's "unified approach to delivering thoughtful strategy and smart technology to craft high-quality digital engagements for clients."

His advice to high school students interested in web design and development:

- "Learn to program in HTML and CSS as soon as possible. The earlier you can start, the better."
- "Look for internship opportunities at local design agencies."
- "Get experience by taking on small projects for your friends and family."

Perhaps Wilson's key to success is that he thoroughly loves what he does and is intrigued by new avenues that are opening. "It's an exciting career to pursue. The industry is constantly changing and it's challenging to try to stay on the cutting edge."

A programmer highlights code for a web development project. Such projects might involve marketing specialists, copywriters, page designers, and many other professionals.

the site. Like programmers, they must be detail-conscious: a tiny error in HTML programming code can wreck a webpage.

COMPUTER AND INFORMATION RESEARCH SCIENCE

Information research scientists in this advanced field come up with new approaches to high technology, pressing the envelope to get the best benefits. Research scientists study problems that computers can solve in science, medicine, business, and other areas. They invent fresh solutions or come up with new ways to use existing software. Some of their work results in faster computing, more efficient computer networks, and better security.

Some research scientists invent new programming languages. Scientists also improve instruction sets (algorithms) that tell computers how to function. They test software and study the results.

Research scientists work for the federal government, systems design companies, software publishers, colleges and universities, and research and development firms. Most have doctorates in computer science, computer engineering, or a related category. Undergraduate and master's degrees suffice for jobs in some sectors. Research scientists with Ph.D. degrees are in especially high demand. Applicants who want to work in a specific industry or profession fare better if they also have knowledge or experience in that field.

The job market is expected to grow 15 percent by 2022—faster than the overall job growth average. Especially rapid growth is expected in jobs related to robotics, data mining, and cybersecurity. Computer scientists may advance to high-level roles as computer and information systems managers.

Aspiring computer and information research scientists must be analytical, critical, logical problem solvers. They should be detail-oriented and able to communicate well.

OTHER CAREERS

Computer and IT managers as well as project managers are high-level technical officers. They help plan and oversee many or all of an organization's computer systems. Most managers have bachelor's or higher degrees.

Computer network architects design and develop local and wide area networks as well as intranets. Some networks are local, others international. Technology architects generally hold bachelor's degrees.

Information security analysts have one primary responsibility: to secure their employing organization's data against cyberattacks. This role has become increasingly important in the twenty-first century. Security analysts usually have degrees in computer science and programming and experience in information technology and administration.

Database administrators are in charge of storing and organizing data for their employer organizations. Data might include documents or financial and sales records. Administrators ensure that officials and employees can access the information reliably and securely. They typically have management information systems (MIS) degrees.

Network and computer systems administrators are in charge of the daily operation of computer networks. It's vital for an organization to keep its network components functioning together smoothly. Most systems administrators have bachelor's degrees in computer or information science or at least post–high school certificates.

Some software developers and programmers take up full-time or part-time careers as postsecondary teachers at technical schools or colleges. These roles usually require a degree in the subject area.

CHAPTER SIX

LANDING A JOB

Most students in high school and junior high aren't immediately concerned with finding a job in software development and programming. (A few students, though, have already worked after hours performing computer-related tasks for local businesses and organizations.) While in school, once again, STEM studies and activities are key. Students should obtain instruction and experience that will be useful when they do set out in their career pursuits.

Basic job search procedures are much the same for high school students seeking a part-time job and for college graduates entering the workforce full-time. The first thing to do is begin building their résumés.

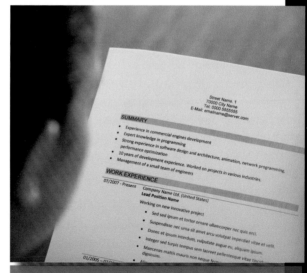

Every job seeker should have a résumé to present to prospective employers. Even if a young person has no work experience, it can show the person's interest in the job.

WHAT IS A RÉSUMÉ AND WHY DO I NEED ONE NOW?

Your résumé is the description of yourself that you will present to potential employers. You will update it regularly throughout your life. For preliminary job applications, it's one of two essential items to help make that all-important positive first impression with a would-be employer. The other item is a short but engaging cover letter.

If you haven't already started your résumé, do it now. Even before you obtain your first part-time job, you can create a basic résumé that describes your personal interests, strong subjects in school, involvement in school and community activities, and tentative career interests.

Your résumé can include the following:

- Your full contact information and a link to your website or blog, if you have one.
- Employment objective. For the moment, your job objective may be merely to obtain a part-time or temporary position performing any type of work for a local web design agency, computer store, or other business. (Any previous work history will be a plus in career advancement.) As you obtain experience, proceed in your education, and narrow you career interests, your objective will become more focused and full-time/long-term.

- Qualifications. Examples: knowledge of an app programming language, understanding of simple web page creation, or computer classes in school.
- Experience. Naturally, you should concentrate on computer-related experience such as simple app programming, blogging, or helping design and build a club website. Until you acquire that kind of background, your résumé can include any experience that indicates your ability to communicate, ability to interact and work with people, and willingness to take on a wide variety of assignments.
- Current grade in school or educational level attained, with your grade point average (GPA).

When applying for a job in person, you'll present your résumé for the hiring representative to review and place on file. When applying by mail or e-mail, you need to accompany the résumé with a cover letter. Your cover letter should include these items, briefly phrased:

- A statement of your interest in a specific job with the employer.
- An explanation of why you're interested in that particular job with that particular employer and what you believe would make you a good fit.

The cover letter should include your contact information in the header. In the closing, you should thank the reviewer for his or her time and consideration.

INTERVIEW WITH A PASSION

When you're invited to a job interview, you should go prepared. Learn all you can about the job and place of employment. This information will let the interviewer know that you're a serious candidate. It will also give you confidence as you answer questions, show your understanding of what the job entails, and explain why you want to work there.

Interviewers are impressed by candidates who demonstrate a passion for working at that location targeting a particular job. If you can convey a desire to work for that employer—not just anywhere—you've scored a plus.

WHERE TO APPLY

Searching online, you may identify local computer and web-related agencies, local and distant businesses and industries, government agencies, and research organizations that have potential openings.

High school students can apply for part-time jobs at technology stores or in the computer departments of office supply and department stores. They may find employment assisting local computer technicians.

Some high school students who are computer savvy jump-start their own careers. One way is to establish a reputation as a techie for local nonprofit organizations and businesses. You might begin by volunteering to create and maintain a website or blog for free. Then, for a modest wage, you can offer to learn new business programs and useful apps and teach them to office staff, thus saving the organization training time. Some teens have become go-to troubleshooters, making themselves available to solve computer problems for small businesses after school and on weekends. Advertisements, circulars, and e-mail marketing campaigns may turn up a surprising volume of business.

Meanwhile, you should begin learning about how the software industry works. Read magazine articles about new software and development news. Check out books on software design, website design and development, and programming. You can begin career networking by following noted bloggers (many of them are columnists for computer periodicals) and occasionally posting questions and comments at their blogs. Join computer-related organizations.

College students can find internships at software companies large and small and possibly in the information technology departments of area businesses. An internship may not pay a handsome salary or offer employment benefits, but it will provide priceless experience and be an important credential on a résumé.

It's important to let employed friends and adult acquaintances know that you're job hunting. They may be aware of openings or possibilities and can tell you whom to contact.

DO YOU NEED A COLLEGE DEGREE?

Not all software developers and programmers have college degrees or certificates from technical training programs. Some successful professionals are essentially self-taught. However, even long-time veterans who carved their own careers during the early years of the computer revolution have benefited from classes, books, seminars, and online training sessions. They understand that in order to advance, they must constantly broaden their knowledge and keep abreast of new technologies.

With each passing year, more employers are requiring job candidates to have computer-related degrees. Competition for jobs is becoming tougher as more applicants entering the workplace are degree holders. Still, jobs are available for exceptional young applicants with high school diplomas.

Elisha Chirchir, a software developer and author of the *Simple Developer* blog, writes that "passion and commitment" are the

A college degree may prove invaluable to someone seeking a computer software career. At the same time, some teens have built upon their own unique experiences to start careers without college degrees.

most important qualities in pursuing any career, and a degree may not be essential. Regardless, you definitely need to learn your craft. Chirchir advises learning and diligently practicing at least one programming language ("the more the better") such as Python or C++. "Make mistakes, find solutions, and repeat!"

Particularly useful experiences, Chirchir writes, are to write programs for yourself and participate in open source development projects. "You need to show [employers] that you are capable. You have a better chance if you can show them your portfolio than a fresh college graduate who has none."

Many other advisers concur. In some career categories, a college degree is practically required. But in software technology, employers are more focused on seeing just what a job candidate can do. Where and how the applicant obtained the necessary skills and knowledge—at a university, through an online educational program, or by reading books and learning design techniques and programming languages at home—isn't the main concern. What matters is the evidence that he or she can produce excellent designs or write and perfect solid program code.

Regardless of the educational level you attain before beginning your career, learning never ends. As noted in previous sections, the best opportunities for advancement will belong to those who take continuing education courses and learn new design techniques, programming languages, and technology tools. Continuing education is important in all professions. It's especially important in the fast-changing world of software development, programming, and related careers.

WIDE-OPEN OPPORTUNITIES

A short distance from Google's headquarters in California is a semi-secret lab where Google technologists are encouraged to try for the impossible. The director, Astro Teller, explains that at the Google X facility, innovators are asked to improve a product or system not by 10 percent—a typical ambition of computer scientists—but by 10 *times*. In other words, rather than develop a car that can stretch fuel economy to 50 miles (80.5 kilometers) per gallon of gas, why not try for 500 miles (805 kilometers) per gallon?

Google X has already produced eyewear (Google Glass) that wearers can use to access and view their smart phone information on a tiny screen at the corner of their field of vision. They can issue voice commands to the phone and take pictures of what's in front of them.

More ambitious projects include a self-driving car, a wind power operation, and an airborne drone delivery service. A life-sciences division is working on concepts for improving the quality of life.

Google's Astro Teller challenges software developers to fail. His philosophy: by failing, they learn. They can find remedies to their mistakes and come up with mind-boggling successes.

Not many computer software companies strive for such ambitious achievements with an extraordinarily high risk of failure. But it's the kind of approach that has made Google an Internet pioneer. Teller says it's why some of the best technologists in the world are eager to work at Google X. "I'm asking them to be responsibly irresponsible," he told a BBC interviewer. Project teams are prodded to pursue incredible objectives, experiment, and start over again when they fail. "I think being afraid to fail is almost a guarantee of a glass ceiling on the success that can be achieved."

HELPING TO SHAPE A BETTER WORLD

Thanks to the tech world, an auto mechanic in Spokane, Washington, saved something far more valuable than a sputtering car engine. He saved an infant's life.

The mechanic, Jeff Olson, halted his work when an app called PulsePoint, installed on his phone, sounded an alert. He read the memo, which called for immediate cardio-pulmonary resuscitation (CPR) at a retail store two blocks away. Olson ran to the scene. A customer's month-old baby had stopped breathing and the store clerk frantically called 911.

Olson immediately administered CPR to the child. The infant began breathing normally.

PulsePoint, a free app for assisting emergency medical workers and volunteers, is one of thousands of emerging computer programs and apps that are changing the world for the better.

Apps can turn your smartphone into a heart rate and blood pressure monitoring device. They can keep restless infants occupied, teaching them computer skills long before they enter kindergarten. Security apps can track a lost or stolen mobile device and prevent unauthorized users from seeing the owner's private information.

Other apps aid the environment. For example, drivers with empty seats in their vehicles can find people in need of a ride along the same route. Ride sharing is an important way to reduce carbon emissions.

Desktop software and mobile apps represent two flourishing career fields for developers and programmers. Another expanding area is cloud computing with software that resides on the Internet. As stated earlier, cloud programs are housed on remote server computers. End users don't have the software installed on their desktops or mobile PCs. Rather, they log onto the server to create, share, and store their files.

Cloud computing offers many benefits. Consumers don't have to buy or install program upgrades; developers and programmers make constant improvements and fixes online, in some cases daily. With many cloud systems, the subscriber can use the software with different types of computers. They can go online while traveling and open their stored files rather than carry them on their computer or external hard drives, both of which are vulnerable to loss or theft.

While some developers and programmers are working on powerful new cloud platforms and programs, others are working to make the cloud more secure. Internet-based software presents new op-

APP DEVELOPMENT AS A CAREER LAUNCHING PAD

When mobile apps became the rage in the early 2000s, dozens of new apps were announced weekly. Some of them were developed by teenagers. Brian X. Chen, writing in the *New York Times* ("What It Takes to Be an App Developer," November 17, 2012), mused that in those days, "anyone with a bit of tech-savviness could download some tools, read some books or take some classes and then whip up an app."

If you think up a new app that serves an interesting purpose and you know how to program it, you still can do that. Today, though, you have little likelihood of launching an app that will become widely used or will generate income. There are simply too many apps out there—literally millions already, with more arriving every day. Consumers are drowning in apps.

A teenage student is immersed in her assignment at an "app inventors" workshop camp. Some of today's popular apps—such as Hayden Metsky's pioneering work on Word of the Day in 2008—were created by teens.

While app development is hardly a road to riches for young techno-wizards, it can be a worthwhile endeavor. It offers a glimpse into what a career would be like in software development and programming. It can also be a useful credential when looking for a job. Chen observed, "Even if you don't strike it rich, app development is not a bad skill to learn, and it could open doors at many companies."

Software development kits and programs are available for app developers working with Android, Apple, and other platforms.

portunities for hackers. Software specialists are developing and perfecting systems to thwart cybercriminals.

THE FUTURE BEGINS NOW

Long before they enter the workplace, young people are pushing the envelope of computer technology, exploring new possibilities. As early as junior high school, teens are creating fairly sophisticated apps and desktop programs.

School science projects showcase some of their work. Students are devising spectacular web animations with digital music effects. They're programming video games for blind users. They're programming apps that analyze the readability level of reports they write.

A student sets up her exhibit at a science fair project. Such efforts in high school may be the launching pad for a career in computer design and software development.

Other student-invented apps monitor personal diet and health factors and teach the fundamentals of CPR. Student software innovators are demonstrating how robots can be directed simply by speaking to them in simple commands. Students are also experimenting with improvements in computer science to be applied in such vital fields as medical imaging.

These are just a few of the exciting areas tech-minded students already are exploring. The prospects are infinite for young people interested in software development and programming—and the adventure can begin now.

GLOSSARY

acronym A word created by taking the first letter or letters of words in a phrase, such as GPS (which is defined below).

algorithm A step-by-step method for solving a problem.

Android A touchscreen mobile operating system developed by Google.

beta An almost complete program distributed to testers for fine-tuning.

biometric Pertains to biometry, which is the application of statistics to biology.

build A version of a program under development.

code A set of computer instructions.

compression The reduction of computer data to a smaller size for better speed and management.

curricula The plural form of curriculum; the courses of study offered by a school.

customization The creation of a computer system for a specific group of users, not for general consumers.

cybersecurity Protecting computerized programs and data.

data mining Locating information by searching for patterns in sets of data.

encryption Encoding data so it cannot be accessed by unauthorized people.

flowchart A diagram illustrating how to carry out a procedure step by step.

GPS The acronym for Global Positioning System, a satellite-based navigation system.

intranet A customized computer network for use throughout an organization, based on the Internet model.

iOS A mobile operating system developed by Apple for many of its devices.

iTunes Store Apple's online store where users can download apps and music.

local area network Computers in an office or home that are linked in order to share printers and other common tools.

logo The symbol of a company name designed to give the business visual recognition.

mentor One who guides and counsels a younger person.

multitask To work on two or more tasks simultaneously.

open source A program that can run on computers that have different operating systems.

operating system The underlying software that controls how a class of computers operate generally.

pathing Plotting the shortest way to perform an action in a computer program.

plugin Add-on software that expands the powers of another program.

portfolio A selection of one's best work to show prospective employers.

robotics The technology of automated machines.

scripting language A high-level programming language used mainly in web page construction.

typography The appearance of alpha-numeric characters on paper or onscreen.

wide area network A network of computers in multiple locations that are linked to share common resources.

FOR MORE INFORMATION

Canadian Information Processing Society
5090 Explorer Drive, Suite 801
Mississauga, ON L4W 4T9
Canada
(905) 602-1370
Website: http://www.cips.ca/ComputerScience
Canada's association of IT professionals represents
   IT workers. It is involved in shaping public poli-
   cy and professional standards and in community
   assistance.

Computer Science Teachers Association
University of Regina, Department of Computer Science
3737 Wascana Parkway
Regina, SK S4S 0A2
Canada
(306) 585-4632
Website: http://www.cs.uregina.ca/Organizations/
   CSTA
This organization supports and promotes the teaching
   of computer science and related disciplines. The
   association offers opportunities for K–12 teachers
   and students "to better understand the computing
   disciplines and to more successfully prepare themselves to teach and to learn."

Computer Science Zone
340 S. Lemon Avenue, #4284
Walnut, CA 91789
(909) 961-8878

Website: http://www.computersciencezone.org
This is a computer science career site for students and
working professionals. The site is run by Jeremy
Harrison, a systems administrator at the University of
Cincinnati.

IEEE Computer Society
2001 L Street NW, Suite 700
Washington, DC 20036-4928
(202) 371-0101
Website: http://www.computer.org/portal/web/guest/
home
This society sponsors technical conferences, webinars,
publications, and a digital library for computing professionals. It strives to make "the most up-to-date and
advanced information in the computing world easily
accessible" to industry workers.

Scholarships.com, LLC
430 Park Avenue, Suite 3A
Highland Park, IL 60035
Website: http://www.scholarships.com
This organization helps students learn about the financial
aid process and search for scholarships.

Science Buddies
P.O. Box 5038
Carmel, CA 93921
Website: http://www.sciencebuddies.org
This nonprofit group is devoted to building student literacy
in science and technology. It "empowers K-12 stu-
dents, parents, and teachers to quickly and easily find

free project ideas and help in all areas of science from physics to food science and music to microbiology."

U.S. Bureau of Labor Statistics (BLS)
2 Massachusetts Avenue NE, Room 2850
Washington, DC 20212
(202) 691-5200
Website: http://www.bls.gov
The BLS is a U.S. Department of Labor agency that analyzes job descriptions, salaries, growth, demands, trends, and statistics. It publishes the *Occupational Outlook Handbook*, which provides information about hundreds of career fields and specific jobs.

WEBSITES

Because of the changing nature of Internet links, Rosen Publishing has developed an online list of websites related to the subject of this book. This site is updated regularly. Please use this link to access the list:

http://www.rosenlinks.com/PTC/Soft

FOR FURTHER READING

Bonnice, Sherry. *Computer Programmer* (Careers with Character). Broomall, PA: Mason Crest Publishers, 2013.

Featherstone, Mark. *Computer Games Designer* (The Coolest Jobs on the Planet). Mankato, MN: Raintree, 2013.

Freedman, Jeri. *Careers in Computer Science and Programming* (Careers in Computer Technology). New York, NY: Rosen Publishing, 2011.

Freedman, Jeri. *Careers in Computer Support* (Careers in Computer Technology). New York, NY: Rosen Publishing, 2011.

Furgang, Kathy. *Careers in Digital Animation* (Careers in Computer Technology). New York, NY: Rosen Publishing, 2013.

Graham, Ian. *Technology Careers* (In the Workplace). Mankato, MN: Amicus, 2010.

Grayson, Robert. *Careers in Network Engineering* (Careers in Computer Technology). New York, NY: Rosen Publishing, 2011.

Harmon, Daniel E. *Careers in Internet Security* (Careers in Computer Technology). New York, NY: Rosen Publishing, 2011.

Harmon, Daniel E. *First Job Smarts* (Get Smart with Your Money). New York, NY: Rosen Publishing, 2010.

Harmon, Daniel E. *Internship & Volunteer Opportunities for Science and Math Wizards* (A Foot in the Door). New York, NY: Rosen Publishing, 2013.

La Bella, Laura. *Careers in Web Development* (Careers in Computer Technology). New York, NY: Rosen Publishing, 2011.

McGuinness, Daniel. *Cool Careers Without College for People Who Are Really Good at Science & Math* (Cool Careers Without College). New York, NY: Rosen Publishing, 2014.

McGuire, Erin K. *Careers in Database Design* (Careers in Computer Technology). New York, NY: Rosen Publishing, 2011.

Payment, Simone. *Robotics Careers: Preparing for the Future.* New York, NY: Rosen Publishing, 2011.

Poolos, J. *Careers in Online Gaming* (Careers in Computer Technology). New York, NY: Rosen Publishing, 2013.

Scholastic Reference. *Hot Jobs in Video Games* (Cool Careers in Interactive Entertainment). New York, NY: Scholastic Reference, 2010.

Staley, Erin. *Career Building Through Creating Mobile Apps* (Digital Career Building). New York, NY: Rosen Publishing, 2014.

Suen, Anastasia. *Career Building Through Using Search Engine Optimization Techniques* (Digital Career Building). New York, NY: Rosen Publishing, 2014.

Willett, Edward. *Career Building Through Using Digital Design Tools* (Digital Career Building). New York, NY: Rosen Publishing, 2014.

BIBLIOGRAPHY

ABC News/Good Morning America. "Smartphone App Helps Save Washington Baby's Life." September 3, 2014.

BBC Newsnight. "Secret Google Lab 'Rewards Failure.'" January 14, 2014. Retrieved October 2014 (www.bbc.com/news/technology-25883016).

Blizzard Entertainment. "University Relations: Sample Intership Job Description." Retrieved October 2014 (http://us.blizzard.com/en-us/company/careers/university-relations/job-desc/intern/game-programmer.html).

Chen, Brian X. "What It Takes to Be an App Developer." *New York Times*, November 17, 2012. Retrieved October 2014 (www.nytimes.com/2012/11/18/business/what-it-takes-to-be-an-app-developer.html?_r=0).

Chirchir, Elisha. "How to Be a Software Developer Without a College Degree." *Simple Developer* blog, May 13, 2013. Retrieved October 2014 (http://simpledeveloper.com/how-to-be-a-software-developer-without-a-college-degree).

Computer Science Zone. "50 Amazing Computer Science Scholarships." Retrieved October 2014 (www.computersciencezone.org/best-computer-science-scholarships).

Coriander Technologies blog. "The Joel Test Is Antiquated." November 5, 2011. Retrieved October 2014 (www.coriandertech.com/2011/11/05/the-joel-test-is-antiquated).

Harness, Jill. "11 Amazing Science Fair Projects." *Oddee* blog, October 8, 2014. Retrieved October 2014 (www.oddee.com/item_99107.aspx).

Hein, Rich. "10 Programming Languages That Are in Demand by Employers." *Computerworld*, June 11, 2013. Retrieved October 2014 (http://www .computerworld.com/article/2473702/it-careers /97819-Top-10-Programming-Skills-That-Will-Get -You-Hired.html).

Market Wired News Room. "Generation Lonely? 39 Percent of Americans Spend More Time Socializing Online Than Face-to-Face." April 25, 2012. Retrieved October 2014 (http://www.marketwired .com/press-release/generation-lonely-39-percent -americans-spend-more-time-socializing-online-than -face-1648444.htm).

Mielach, David. "Americans Spend 23 Hours Per Week Online, Texting." *Business News Daily*, July 2, 2013. Retrieved October 2014 (www.businessnewsdaily .com/4718-weekly-online-social-media-time.html).

Rowan, David. "Astro Teller of Google[x] Wants to Improve the World's Broken Industries." Wired. co.uk, October 31, 2013. Retrieved October 2014 (www.wired.co.uk/magazine/archive/2013/11/ start/destination-moon).

Spolsky, Joel. "The Joel Test: 12 Steps to Better Code." *Joel on Software* blog, August 9, 2000. Retrieved September 2014 (www.joelonsoftware.com/ articles/fog0000000043.html).

St. George, Donna. "High School Students Are All About Computers But Get Little Instruction in Computer Science." *Washington Post*, April 23, 2014.

Retrieved September 2014 (www.washingtonpost
.com/local/education/high-school-students
-are-all-about-computers-but-get-little-instruction-in
-computer-science/2014/04/23/13979eda-c185
-11e3-bcec-b71ee10e9bc3_story.html).

Thomas Public Relations. "Get Focused & Relax With
Zen180 Meditation & Brain Enhancement App."
Press release, September 8, 2014. Retrieved
September 2014 (www.thomas-pr.com/zen180/
zen180release.html).

Zolyak, Adam. "How Long Does It Take to Build a
Mobile Application?" *Segue Technologies* blog,
May 10, 2013. Retrieved October 2014 (www
.seguetech.com/blog/2013/05/10/how-long
-build-mobile-application).

INDEX

A

applications developers
  what they do, 28
apps
  development time, 29–30
  as the foundation of a career,
    65–66

C

career paths
  profiles of some, 16
classes
  which to take for a program-
    ming career, 15, 22, 24
college degrees
  deciding whether to pursue
    one, 60–61
computer and information
    research scientists
  what they do, 52–53
computer network architects
  career overview, 53
computer programs
  capabilities of, 8–9, 10–11,
    63–64, 66–67
computer systems analysts
  what they do, 43–45

computer terms
  glossary of, 18–19
cover letter, 56, 57

D

database administrators
  career overview, 53–54

E

entertainment and gaming apps
  types of, 13–14

G

Google X, 62–63

I

information security analysts
  career overview, 53
Internet job searches
  how to tailor, 23
internships, 18, 20–22, 23, 24,
    40, 51, 59
interviews, 20, 38, 58
IT project managers
  what they do, 28, 31

J

jobs
  finding, 23, 55
  where to apply, 58–59
"Joel Test," 37, 38–39

N

network and computer systems
    administrators
  career overview, 54

P

programming
  career outlook, 42
  internships in, 20–21
  skills needed for, 39–41
  what programmers do,
    34–37, 39

R

résumé, 55, 56–57

S

scholarships, 16–18, 24
software development
  career outlook, 32–33

internships in, 18, 20
skills needed for, 31–32, 33
what developers do, 26–28, 31
work environment, 31
software support
  internships in, 21
  what support staff does,
    45–47
STEM classes, 15, 39, 55
systems developers
  what they do, 27–28

T

teaching, 54

V

voice technology, 12–13

W

web design, development, and
    maintenance
  internships in, 21–22
  tips from a web designer,
    50–51
  what web developers do,
    47–49, 52

ABOUT THE AUTHOR

Daniel E. Harmon is the author of more than ninety books. His career studies volumes include *Careers in Internet Security* (Careers in Computer Technology) from Rosen Publishing. A veteran editor and writer, he has contributed thousands of articles to national and regional magazines and newspapers. He edits *The Lawyer's PC*, a newsletter devoted to the use of computers and related technology in law practice. Harmon has designed and maintained a variety of websites. He lives in Spartanburg, South Carolina.

PHOTO CREDITS